Date: 2/3/12

J 355.41 MEY
Meyer, Jared.
Working in a war zone :
military contractors /

EXTREME CAREERS™

WORKING IN A WAR ZONE
Military Contractors

Jared Meyer

rosen publishing's
rosen
central®

New York

To Seth and Samara for allowing me to develop my interpretation and negotiation skills at such a young age

Published in 2007 by The Rosen Publishing Group, Inc.
29 East 21st Street, New York, NY 10010

Library of Congress Cataloging-in-Publication Data

Meyer, Jared.
Working in a war zone : military contractors / Jared Meyer.
p. cm. — (Extreme careers)
Includes bibliographical references and index.
ISBN-13: 978-1-4042-0959-6
ISBN-10: 1-4042-0959-X (library binding)
1. Public contracts—United States—Vocational guidance—Juvenile litera-
ture. 2. Contracting out—United States—Vocational guidance—Juvenile
literature. 3. Contractors—United States—Vocational guidance—Juvenile literature. 4. Defense industries—United States—Vocational
guidance—Juvenile literature. I. Title. II. Series.
HD3861.U6M49 2006
355.4'1—dc22

2006016510

Manufactured in the United States of America

On the cover: A military contractor working for the U.S. armed forces in Iraq.

Contents

Introduction

Though they often work in war zones, there are many different types of military contractors, some of whom are stationed within the heat of battle and others whom are not. For the purposes of this book, we'll look at several very different types of military contractors.

The government and the military often hire military contractors for certain jobs that they want done by professionals. Military contractors are offered opportunities to provide goods and services either directly to the government or military or to other groups that these organizations wish to support, such as foreign countries or foreign militaries. They're hired to work on projects, programs, or missions for certain periods of time.

This book covers a few high-profile, yet nontraditional, career opportunities available to military contractors.

For example, during wartime, the government may send the military to a foreign country to investigate the whereabouts of weapons of mass destruction or perhaps the assassination attempts on a powerful leader. Given that these military personnel may not know the language, language interpreters may be hired as contractors to assist.

Yes, interpreters are also military contractors. While the specific job of language interpretation is not necessarily dangerous, the working environments can make this type of contractor's work unique, extreme, risky, and thrilling. Acting as an outsider in a foreign country without a stable government or any upheld laws may just be the beginning of working in a dangerous environment as a military contractor. Random gunfire and rioting, among other unyielding dangers, can make working as an interpreter an extremely demanding and exciting career.

Military contractors in the form of humanitarian and civic action workers may also be called upon to assist in the rebuilding of war-torn areas. They may offer their services on behalf of the government to rebuild bridges and roads or dig wells for fresh water. Those professionals with a background and experience in medicine may be

Military contractors can promote their products and services by networking at industry tradeshows, such as the Marine West Military Exposition in Camp Pendleton, CA.

able to provide aid to people hurt by gunfire, explosions, or contaminated water.

As you can see, there are many different types of military contractors. Despite their differences, they all share the challenges of working thrilling jobs, often in dangerous areas. Even with these challenges, however, military contractors continue their efforts in serving the military, the government, and their country in any number of ways.

What Are Military Contractors?

1

Military contractors, as their title describes, are people who are contracted, or hired, by the U.S. government to provide any number of products or services to the military. They are people who work independently of the military but perform a variety of jobs for the government and the armed forces. Military contractors are often portrayed in the news as people who rebuild war-torn areas or manufacture fighter jets for the U.S. Air Force. While the people who perform these duties are indeed military contractors, there are hundreds of other contractors that you rarely hear about.

There are two basic types of military contractor: corporations and individuals. Corporate contractors can make products, such as aircraft, or provide services, such as security, to the military. Individuals who are military contractors, often called independent contractors, are people who offer their goods or services to the military on their own as independent business people without the backing of a company.

Both independent and corporate military contractors can enjoy the benefits of being in the industry. Some people may start off working for a company and then go off on their own after they feel they've had enough experience and training. Others may start off as independent contractors and then decide that they would like more job security by working for a company other than their own. In either case, there are benefits and drawbacks to each.

Independent Contractors

While many people, regardless of whether they are military contractors, prefer the stability and commitment of being an employee of a company, there are also those people who like to be self-employed and who desire a different work style and quality of life. In the world of military contractors, these people are independent contractors.

Independent contractors can be hired for any number of jobs, including supplying armor to this heavy equipment transport (HET) vehicle at Camp Anaconda, Iraq.

An independent contractor is an independent businessperson. Independent contractors can start virtually any kind of military contractor business that they want. If they have the desire and the know-how to succeed, they can start one that allows them to offer any one of a variety of products or services to clients within the military that they might have expertise in.

If they manage their business well, independent contractors can have great success. The independent may have the chance to expand the types of products or services he or she offers if good business decisions are made. However, it all depends on the goals of the individual. Short-term and long-term goals will vary, and each decision that is made will affect success, just as it is with any type of business.

Also like other self-employed individuals, independent contractors are the ones responsible for every aspect of their entire business. They must be effective managers and very organized. The business is theirs, and they have no long-term boss to serve, only clients and occasionally short-term direct supervisors.

Usually, independent contractors don't have supervisors to turn to for assistance when the going gets tough. They may be all on their own at times during their day-to-day work. However, it is not uncommon for independent contractors to work together. They can pool their ideas and resources and start a partnership. Partnerships are good since the risks are shared. The rewards, however, are shared as well.

Independent contractors usually have certain qualities that make them different from the traditional career-minded professional who works for a corporation.

Independent contractors are often highly motivated, risk-taking decision makers who like to be on their own. They are dedicated and hardworking since their careers may demand fifty to seventy hours a week from them.

Independent contractors also tend to be highly organized. They need to be since they are responsible for running each of the different areas of their career, such as networking, partnerships, and marketing. Though they are responsible for handling most aspects of their business, they usually choose self-employment because they believe that they will be happier and therefore more successful with the freedom that comes from working on their own.

Risks and Rewards of Independence

There are risks and rewards to being an independent contractor. Independent contractors, more so than corporate contractors, can face personal, financial, and career risks when they work on their own business ventures. They know that they can possibly lose all of the money, as well as many of the hours of work, they invest in their career. Additionally, they usually don't receive many of the benefits they might enjoy if they worked for a company, such as health care, insurance, or investment plans.

Although being an independent contractor can be risky, there are many rewards for being self-employed. Independence is among the most important. Independent contractors have the freedom to make their own decisions about their business, and they can have an enjoyable lifestyle and career by working free of corporate restraints, such as rigid working hours and limited time off. In addition, if the right decisions are made and if career efforts are successful, a good amount of money can be made as an independent contractor.

Corporate Military Contractors

Businesses or corporations that provide goods or services to the government or military are another type of military contractor. These organizations create and maintain mutually beneficial contracts with the government or military. Within these military contractor organizations are people who share similar interests and talents, such as providing security or manufacturing military aircraft.

Corporate military contractors, such as the firm Blackwater, offer solutions for many larger scale military needs such as providing advanced military helicopters.

Corporate military contractors are often large companies that provide such goods and services as aircraft, weapons, military tools, and even staff to the government.

There are a good number of these organizations, which are often called upon by the American government to provide solutions to challenges the military can't handle on its own. Issues such as terrorism, working with war-torn nations, and maintaining America's own security may be faced better by contractors that specialize in these areas. Working with qualified defense manufacturers has helped America maintain one of the strongest military forces in the world.

The Military Industry

Within the military, there are new jobs being created for contractors all the time. These jobs are influenced in large part by the government's need for new technology. For example, if new Global Positioning Systems (GPS) are needed to allow the military to better locate and strike its targets, there will be a greater demand for military contractors with a background in computers, programming, and satellite systems to produce the devices. Another instance might be if a defense manufacturer completely redesigned an aircraft. Contractors serving as experimental test pilots might be hired by the military to test the new equipment if their expertise is needed.

As you can see, there are many different types of jobs for military contractors within the industry. Some jobs can be routine while others can be exciting and extreme. The bottom line, though, is that when it comes to a

career as a military contractor, there are two factors applicants must consider: whether they want to work with the military and what life would be like serving as a military contractor. Each area of the military industry is different. Some military contractors have to work

Being a military contractor means taking on any number of jobs, such as loading the latest satellite-guided bombs aboard fighter planes.

in highly dangerous areas under intense levels of pressure and perform extensive amounts of physical labor in extreme climates, such as the Arctic or the desert. This all depends on which division of the military a person works for.

The defense industry is made up of several different divisions. A couple of the divisions that work with military contractors are the armed forces and the U.S. government.

The U.S. Armed Forces

The U.S. armed forces include the U.S. Army, Navy, Air Force, Marine Corps, and Coast Guard. Within these organizations are multiple departments with various objectives and missions. The armed forces mainly serve to protect and defend individuals, groups of people, or other countries. At other times, their responsibilities are to provide aid and recovery to people after they have been attacked by terrorists, struck by destructive forces of nature, or experienced any other type of catastrophic event.

Most recently, areas of Iraq have been ravaged by war. Contractors working in this environment to evaluate the damage face potentially devastating danger. For instance, the aftereffects of this damage add to the obstacles in their way. Buildings may collapse at any time. Pipes that were constructed to transport gas may ignite and explode. These are some of the dangers

This car bomb explosion shows that the working environment of military contractors can turn from a peaceful and quiet city street into a chaotic and dangerous war zone.

that those who work as contractors for the U.S. armed forces are trained to expect and overcome when working in war zones.

The U.S. Government

Governmental organizations such as the Department of Defense have military contractors work for them as well. The government uses the products and services of military contractors so it doesn't have to personally invest in the technology and talent itself. Using the resources of military contractors in this way is called outsourcing. It's often both more efficient and effective for the government to outsource certain needs rather than provide them by itself.

On the Job

Though there are practically hundreds of different types of military contractor careers, this chapter focuses on three that are a little different and more interesting than others: language interpreters, humanitarian workers, and test pilots. These are good examples of the variety of exciting and extreme careers available in the field.

Language Interpreters

A language interpreter is a person who acts as an intermediary between two people sharing a conversation in two different languages. Interpreters are fluent in both languages and are able to converse with both parties at the same time. Because of this skill, they are extremely

Language interpreters are often assigned to missions within war zones and other areas where communication is difficult yet vital to getting the job done.

important to the government when it is involved in international affairs.

Responsibilities of an interpreter may include translating conversations and documents. Interpreters may also be called upon to interpret a speech at a conference. In this case, the interpreter may sit in a closed-off area, such as a soundproof booth, to prevent disruption or difficulty for those listening to the interpretation. The interpreter would speak into a microphone, and an audio system would allow the audience members who wish to hear the interpretation of the presentation to listen via headphones.

The demand for conference interpreters is strong at global organizations such as the United Nations (UN), the European Union, and the African Union. These organizations are made up of people who speak a variety of languages. Without the help of interpreters, there would be no conversations between people who speak different languages. While these types of inter-preters may be employed by the UN directly, military contractors that are hired by the government or military to act as interpreters are not as fortunate to work in comfortable and secure environments.

Military contracted interpreters may be as educated as those who work within the UN, but they will have additional training in survival since they are often hired to work in war zones. These interpreters may be flown to cities in several different countries in a single month.

While military contracted interpreters may have exciting jobs, there remain life-threatening risks in the profession. Gunfire, explosions, and human suffering exist in environments where governments may be unestablished and people have to fend for themselves. While soldiers may attempt to provide relief to devastated areas, interpreters may be sent to assist the soldiers to investigate terrorism, assassination attempts on political leaders, or the mass shipment of narcotics, among other evils.

Interpreters control the missions of the soldiers who protect them in that they must precisely communicate what is told to them. Some areas of a war zone may be worse than others, but most interpreters simply cannot prepare for specific conflicts that occur. When will the next bomb go off? Will it be nearby? Who is concealing a weapon? These are some of the thoughts that run through the minds of military contracted interpreters in war zones. This uncertainty can cause a lot of stress and end up compromising the safety of the group the interpreter travels with. That is why military contractors in this capacity are hired with the understanding and ability that they must face the risks of working in a war zone.

Locating water that is healthy to drink in communities is one common objective of humanitarian and civil action workers, such as this employee for corporate military contractor Bechtel.

Humanitarian and Civic Action Workers

Humanitarian and civic action workers are often military contractors who work with others in need of assistance due to the effects of both man-made and natural disasters. The term "humanitarian" means compassionate and kind-hearted, and the term "civic" refers to the community, town, or city where help is offered. According to the Department of Defense, its Humanitarian Civic Assistance (HCA) program offers struggling countries with limited resources the opportunity to benefit from important and helpful activities such as rebuilding after a disaster, health-care treatment, and water purity maintenance.

Organizations within the armed forces such as the U.S. National Guard and Special Operations provide humanitarian and civic actions worldwide. Military contractors may be called in to assist the armed forces with the rebuilding of a community or preparing it for an upcoming potential disaster such as a hurricane, especially if the military is unable to staff enough of its own to handle the mission. At other times, these humanitarian and civic action workers are needed to help the people living in war zones. Even with fighting taking place, these contractors can work long hours of hard physical labor. While it may be a daunting task to rebuild in such dangerous areas, military contractors offer their services to assist as best as they can.

Humanitarian assistance can include feeding the hungry, preventing the spread of disease or conflict, preventing the loss of or damage to property, and most important, saving lives. It may also include road and school construction and digging wells for access to water—this is considered the rebuilding of infrastructures.

The Rebuilding of Infrastructures

Military contractors may be called upon to assist in the rebuilding of communities in the wake of a

Maintaining infrastructures, such as this power plant in Baghdad, Iraq, is important to the rejuvenation of war-torn areas. Electrical engineers are assigned to these jobs.

tragedy such as a natural disaster or war. If an elementary or high school were damaged or completely destroyed, military contractors would be needed to assist in its reconstruction. Furthermore, the contractors could also help teach the children in the community should the original teachers be unavailable at the time. This of course would depend on the qualifications of the military contractors. The more skills they have, the more opportunities they may have to make a greater impact on the communities where they are sent to help.

Preparing for Disaster

Consider what would happen if the mayor of a major metropolis received a notification that the city was the potential target of a bioterrorist. Bioterrorism, the act of using lethal chemicals to kill people and create fear within a community, could lead to a man-made disaster, wiping out hundreds or thousands of innocent people.

In preparation of this unfortunate occurrence, military contractors may be requested to support the area's efforts in protecting its citizens from harm in any number of ways. They could offer medical vaccinations to the citizens of the city. While visiting the city, they could also provide their services to assist in the preparation of the potential disaster. It would depend on the objectives of their mission.

Well Digging

In some countries, people may not be fortunate enough to live in an environment with common luxuries like abundant running water that is safe to drink and reliable waste management services. Should a war or disaster hit an area such as this, there is a possibility that water may no longer be accessible, reliable, or healthy to consume. Military contractors would be able to teach the citizens how to find fresh water and perhaps how to even filtrate it to ensure that it is healthy enough for consumption.

Often, the best solution to finding good water during times of hardship is to dig a well rather than rely on existing rivers, streams, or water systems. Military contractors sent to do this job would be trained in knowing where to dig and whether the water found is good for the community. While digging wells isn't the sole service of any one humanitarian or civic action worker, military contractors with a background in construction and

When water is temporarily compromised or even completely lost in a community, military contractors are called upon to dig wells and revive the community with fresh water.

engineering would be able to offer their skills as well as their physical labor in finding fresh water for communities.

Experimental Test Pilots

Experimental test pilots are sometimes contracted by the military, too. They are essentially hired to fly both brand-new as well as current models of airplanes that have been modified so the military can safely use them. They are also required to make calculations based on their experience while flying to determine if any further modifications should be made to the current technology on board. During their flights and especially upon landing, the test pilots have to document their thoughts and concerns based on their professional opinions. After their flights and time spent documenting them, they submit technical reports to their supervisors or clients.

Sometimes, if there is inadequate time for testing the aircraft in a peaceful environment, testing may have to be done in regions that are in or near dangerous war zones. For example, if new flight technology is added to an existing aircraft within a war zone, an experimental test pilot may be called upon to test out the new technical

Experiential test pilots not only risk that their test planes will malfunction but also that they will be shot down by enemy forces when flying in war zones.

enhancements before it is used. When this is done, the risk of danger increases because the test pilot not only has to deal with the possibility of a technical malfunction but also the danger of being a target of the enemy.

While the armed services may recruit their own pilots from within their organizations, military contractors may be requested to assist or even to lead the projects. Experimental test pilots not only have to be qualified to fly planes, they must also be trained in mathematics and communications to effectively administer the testing phase of new or modified planes.

While there may be a limited amount of certified test pilots in North America, there is one organization called the Society of Experimental Test Pilots, which allows a group of individuals to come together to engage in dialogues about their experiences. That is, of course, unless the information is classified. Another organization for test pilots is the Experimental Aircraft Association. According to its Web site, it is the "Leader in Recreational Aviation" and acts as an organization for people who love anything to do with aviation and those who wish to work in this military contractor field.

The Benefits

Being a military contractor is not a well-publicized career given that there are so many jobs that can fall under the category. There are opportunities as inter-preters, humanitarian and civic action workers, and experimental test pilots, as well as many others that aren't covered in this book. Despite the numerous and exciting opportunities within the military contractor field, the most popular ones are usually those with the best benefits, such as being able to travel the world, learn about new cultures, help people, and most important, save lives.

World Travel

Some people spend their entire lives in one part of the world, never setting foot in another country or even another part of their own country. Perhaps they've never had the opportunity or ability to travel out of their area. Maybe they are simply quite comfortable living where they grew up. Staying put in one place is satisfying to many people. Traveling isn't for everyone. For others, though, having the chance to explore the world can be very exciting. For those people who are interested in travel, being able to see the world, even if they may have to go to dangerous areas, is definitely a perk of the job of military contractor.

Depending on the requirements of their job and objectives of their projects or missions, military contractors may be able to see all different parts of the world. An interpreter based in New York City who is hired to work directly for the United Nations may not have many opportunities to travel if he or she works only in New York. However, a military contracted interpreter hired by the government could be needed at a series of global conferences taking place in major cities like Tokyo, Rome, and Athens, so he or she will definitely be traveling the world.

Unfortunately, based on the few opportunities available to work in such safe environments, there may only be a

Disasters can happen anywhere, and there will always be military contractors willing and ready to travel to those areas even if they are thousands of miles from home.

few conferences like this for an interpreter to work each year. Alternatively, there will often be opportunities for military contractors to act as interpreters in war zones, traveling from one devastated area to another. While this may not be the type of world travel where one would bring his or her family, it can still be a pretty exciting experience for people who are looking for adventure.

Perhaps during the months an interpreter is free from global travel, he or she may work within one country traveling between regions. If an interpreter who is traditionally hired by the government or military only during the summers wants to get more work in the industry, he or she may look into getting involved with organizations that send interpreters all over the country for special events or localized disasters. When it comes to humanitarian and civic action workers, these military contractors will often go where damage, such as from wars or natural disasters, has been done or is expected to occur. This could be within America, such as in New Orleans, Louisiana, after Hurricanes Rita and Katrina, or as far from America as Sri Lanka, as in the wake of the South Asian tsunami that struck that country in December 2004.

Learning About New Cultures and People

America is often described as a melting pot of people of many different races who come from vastly different countries and cultures. Celebrating diversity can be beautiful if the opportunity to meet and get to know

World travel is one of the benefits of being a military contractor. Being able to see the world is a rare and exciting opportunity for most people.

different people is available. In America's large cities, like New York and Los Angeles, people can't escape diversity. However, in many less populated parts of the country, diversity is not as prevalent and people unfortunately don't have the opportunity to learn about different customs and religions despite America's multi-culturalism.

Military contractors, especially those who come from small towns or cities with little diversity, have the chance to learn about new cultures and people because of their jobs. If a military contractor, acting as an inter-preter for example, is flown to Africa to assist in the development of a new form of government, imagine what would lie ahead for that person. He or she could be immersed not only in an area where everyone speaks a different language but also in African music, art, litera-ture, performance, and food.

In 2001, Hurricane Michelle hit the country of Honduras. Thankfully, there were minimal casualties, but 25,000 people had to be evacuated from their homes. While humanitarian and civic action workers helped those in need, there were some military contractors who probably arrived in this country for the very first time. If they were unfamiliar with Hondurans or their way of life, these military contractors would have to learn pretty quickly. There wasn't much time to do this. Being placed in a new environment without much preparation can be quite an adventure.

Working for a Good Cause

In a perfect world, everyone's job would contribute to benefiting all of the people in the world in some capacity. In reality, though, some jobs simply don't provide as much of a humanitarian impact as others. However, when it comes to the careers of military contractors, it's hard for their work not to be considered noble for all the charitable contributions the job offers to those in need.

Consider a military contracted interpreter who travels to a far-off country to assist the U.S. military in the development of a new local government and the rebuilding of a city that suffered from being in the center of a war zone. With the contributions of contractors, the community can be rebuilt and renewed relatively quickly because of the contractors' work acting as intermediaries between the citizens and the military.

Whether it is rebuilding a well or rebuilding a government, military contractors' efforts are done in the best interest of the people they are sent to serve.

Think about the good work another interpreter could do by acting as a mediator during conflict resolution hearings between two feuding groups that speak different languages. Military-contracted interpreters could be called in to assist in the communication between these two parties.

Military contractors who travel to devastated areas to rebuild roads and schools, to help provide medical treatment to people, and to dig for hours at a time to

Rebuilding homes and constructing new ones can rarely be accomplished without the help of military contractors, such as these in Sri Lanka after the 2004 tsunami.

find fresh water that is healthy enough to drink, certainly do good work for good causes.

On another level, experimental test pilots can be some of the most giving military contractors working today. Depending on the extensiveness of their flight tests, they may have to risk their lives making sure that new or modified aircraft are safe enough for the armed forces that protect America.

While there will always be perks available to the individuals working as military contractors and great benefits to the people, cities, and countries that reap the rewards of their contributions, these jobs aren't always located in the best of work environments, as we'll see.

The Challenges of the Job

4

As with most jobs, there are some less appealing aspects of being a military contractor. There are the usual employment hassles like having to sometimes work with difficult people and having too much to do with not enough time to do it. However, these are minor issues compared to the great challenges and life-threatening dangers that military contractors may face on the job.

Whereas traditional employees may have to suffer through long, boring meetings, not enough time for a lunch break, and awful commutes to and from work, military contractors, such as interpreters, humanitarian and civic action workers, and experimental test pilots, face a higher level of challenges while working. Three of the biggest challenges that military contractors may experience include the everyday dangers of working in a war zone, emotional suffering from witnessing the devastation and hardship of the people they are trying to help, and illness, pain and suffering, with the potential risk of death. Compared to traditional problems at work, the individuals covered in this book have much bigger worries, but they are trained and committed to accept these challenges and do their jobs anyway.

The Everyday Dangers

Television news broadcasts often show the effects of man-made or natural disasters that people can experience while going about their personal and professional lives. It can happen in most populated areas around the world. Whether a building is bombed and completely destroyed by terrorists, such as on September 11, 2001, or large groups of people are quickly swept away in a flash flood—a sudden rush of water that builds up and swallows whatever is in its path—disasters of all kinds affect thousands of people in our world in some capacity all the time.

Military contractors can be potential victims of such disasters. Imagine if an interpreter hired to represent a

military organization is participating in a conference on global economics. Participation in the event is crucial given that he or she not only assists in the dialogues between the military organization and others, but perhaps because he or she clearly represents the best interests

In a military contractor's line of work, nothing is guaranteed when it comes to safety. Traveling to unstable places such as Baghdad puts their security at risk every day.

of this organization or the entire country's military forces. The interpreter and his or her colleagues may be sitting with or near a group of people that is being targeted by terrorists. In the event that an act of terrorism, like an attempted kidnapping, attack, or bombing of the building occurs, he or she may personally experience the effects of such a tragedy.

What if a humanitarian or civic action worker is in Florida during the state's hurricane season? While assisting the citizens of a small town in Florida in preparing for the potentially dangerous storms in the future, imagine how he or she would feel if the work didn't get finished in time. If a surprise storm hit the location, he or she would be stuck in Florida and would have to experience the very disaster others were being prepared for. Sometimes, military contractors are victims of the disasters they try to save others from.

Emotional Suffering

Of the three types of military contractors covered in this book, humanitarian and civic action workers are most likely to experience emotional suffering from seeing devastation and hardship firsthand. These contractors aren't always sent before disaster or war strikes a town, city, or region. Sometimes, they are deployed immediately after an area has been destroyed.

Military contractors are flown in to help soon after disasters, such as Hurricane Katrina, strike. As a result, they must often face the emotional turmoil that comes with devastation.

While assisting in the rebuilding of a community, these workers will very likely be in contact with wounded or dying people. They may also need to assist people who have lost their families and friends. Under less severe conditions, perhaps the citizens the military contractors have been sent to help are alive and well, but they have nowhere to live. With their homes destroyed and their possessions gone, the devastation and hardship would have just begun for them. The bigger the disaster— whether it is man-made or due to dangerous forces of nature like tsunamis, hurricanes, or tornados—the worse the experience usually is for a military contractor.

How would a humanitarian or civic action worker respond to assisting a woman who has lost her two children due to a tidal wave? Would the worker's background and training keep him or her resilient enough to help support this person who has experienced such a great loss? He or she would need to remain strong not only to do what is best for the woman being helped but also to keep him- or herself from breaking down. It's hard to prepare people for jobs in chaotic environments such as natural disasters and war because the scope of the devastation can sometimes be enormous.

Survival skills for these people in life-threatening environments sometimes include coping emotionally with stress and conflict. Without clear thinking, people in dire situations may find themselves making foolish mistakes in dangerous situations if they allow their emotions to get the best of them. Military contractors are hired to act as leaders and be able to think clearly in all situations to get the job done safely and effectively.

The Risk of Death

The biggest challenge for most military contractors while working on location is staying healthy, preventing personal pain and suffering, and even staying alive. Given the dangerous working conditions that they are sometimes hired to cope with, military contractors can come face-to-face with disease, war, and devastating forces of nature, among other hazards.

The worst risk of all no matter which specific responsibility a military contractor has is the potential risk of death. The situation might require being sent to a foreign country as an interpreter to work with people who are possible assassination targets. A contractor working as a

While abroad in war zones such as Baghdad, contractors must often live in secured quarters because of the constant risk of missile strikes.

humanitarian or civic action worker might have to work in environments that are disease-ridden. A test pilot might have to fly an aircraft that has a chance of malfunctioning or being shot down. Each of these military contractors has one major risk in common, which is death.

This ultimate risk of the job is essentially what makes being a military contractor an exciting job. The value of human life to most people is tremendous, which is why military contractors accept the realities of the dangers they face and commit to their extreme careers. Military contractors hope to contribute to the greater good. Hundreds, thousands, or possibly millions of people can benefit from their work.

Glossary

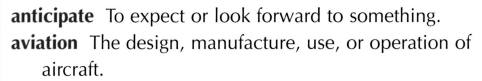

anticipate To expect or look forward to something.

aviation The design, manufacture, use, or operation of aircraft.

casualties Fatalities or victims, usually of war.

civic Of or relating to community or city.

consecutively Happening one after the other.

consultants People who specialize and offer advice in a particular field.

contaminated Polluted.

diversity The state of having variety.

filtration The act of filtering or cleaning of impurities.

humanitarian Of or relating to care or compassion.

interpret To translate one language into another.

marketing The act of promoting one's business.

melting pot A term used to describe racial diversity.

modified Made better.

networking The act of meeting new people and building new business partnerships.

noble Dignified

outsourcing Hiring someone from outside an organization for a job.

scope The range or extent of something.

warfare General fighting or military combat.

For More Information

Center for International Policy
1717 Massachusetts Avenue NW, Suite 801
Washington, DC 20036
(202) 232-3317
e-mail: cip@ciponline.org
Web site: http://www.ciponline.org

**Office of Humanitarian Assistance, Disaster Relief,
  and Mine Action**
Defense Security Cooperation Agency
2800 Defense Pentagon
Washington, DC 20301-2800
(703) 601-3710
Web site: http://www.dsca.mil/programs/HA/HA.htm

United Nations
UN Headquarters
First Avenue at 46th Street
New York, NY 10017
Web site: http://www.un.org

U.S. Department of Defense
5611 Columbia Pike
Falls Church, VA 22041
Web site: http://www.defenselink.mil

Web Sites

Due to the changing nature of Internet links, Rosen Publishing has developed an online list of Web sites related to the subject of this book. This site is updated regularly. Please use this link to access the list:

http://www.rosenlinks.com/ec/wowz

For Further Reading

Bennett, Paul, and George Weber. *War: The World Reacts.* Hauppauge, NY: Barron's Educational Series, 2002.

Griffith, Susan. *Work Your Way Around the World.* Oxford, England: Vacation Work Publications, 2005.

Kruempelmann, Elizabeth. *The Global Citizen: A Guide to Creating an International Life and Career.* Berkeley, CA: Ten Speed Press, 2002.

Lauber, Daniel. *International Job Finder: Where the Jobs Are Worldwide* (International Job Finder). River Forest, IL: Planning Communications, 2002.

Marsh, Carole. *The Adventure Diary of Hannah, the Humanitarian Aid Worker* (Heroes & Helpers). Peachtree City, GA: Gallopade International, 2003.

Pelton, Robert Young. *The Adventurist: My Life in Dangerous Places.* New York, NY: Broadway Books, 2001.

Schumacher, Gerry. *A Bloody Business: America's War Zone Contractors and the Occupation of Iraq.* Osceola, WI: Zenith Press, 2006.

Suen, Anastasia. *Doctors Without Borders.* New York, NY: PowerKids Press, 2003.

Bibliography

Center for International Policy. "Just the Facts: on Humanitarian Civic Assistance." Retrieved February 1, 2006 (http://www.ciponline.org/facts/hca.htm).

Eric Volstad's Web Page. "Test Pilot Stuff." Retrieved February 1, 2006 (http://www.testpilots.com).

Innes, Brian. *International Terrorism*. Broomall, PA: Mason Crest Publishers, 2004.

"National Aeronautics and Space Administration Office of Procurement." Retrieved February 1, 2006 (http://www.hq.nasa.gov/office/procurement/index.html).

Paradis, Adrian A. *Opportunities in Military Careers*. Lincolnwood, IL: VGM Career Horizons, 1999.

Stanley, Sandra Carson. *Women in the Military*. New York, NY: Julian Messner, 1993.

Wikipedia.com. "Defense Contractor." Retrieved February 1, 2006 (http://en.wikipedia.org/wiki/Defense_ contractor).

Wikipedia.com. "Interpreting." Retrieved February 1, 2006 (http://en.wikipedia.org/wiki/Interpreting).

Index

About the Author

Jared Meyer is an author and educator who works with students on improving their decision-making and communication skills. He has written several books on both developing critical-thinking skills and college and career exploration for young readers. Jared works with Monster Worldwide's "Making It Count!" career programs and speaks with large groups of high school students on making personal choices about their college search, college experience, and career, including that of military contractors. He may be contacted at jaredmeyer@makstar.com.

Photo Credits

Cover © Mary Godleski/AP/Wide World Photos; p. 6 © Ann Johansson/Corbis; pp. 10, 30 © Darren McCollester/Getty Images; p. 14, 25 © Marwan Naamani/AFP/Getty Images; pp. 16–17 © PH3 (AW/SW) Joshua Karsten/AFP/Getty Images; p. 19 © Wathiq Khuzaie/Getty Images; p. 22 © Chris Hondros/Getty Images; p. 27 © Scott Nelson/Getty Images; p. 32 © Steve Marcus/Las Vegas Sun/Reuters/Corbis; pp. 36, 42 © Paula Bronstein/Getty Images; p. 38 © Issouf Sanogo/AFP/Getty Images; p. 41 © Joe Raedle/Getty Images; pp. 46–47 © Wisam Sami/AFP/Getty Images; p. 49 © Mario Tama/Getty Images; p. 52 © Benjamin Lowy/Corbis.

Photo Researcher: Hillary Arnold